Countri~~~ ~~ ~~~

KONN_____A

from こんにちは

JAPAN

C. Manica

Special thanks to Nina Kawai-Hopson

こんにちは
Konnichiwa,
I'm Misako Crane.

I'm going to tell you about
my country, Japan!

Japan is in East Asia.

It's an archipelago
(a group of islands).

For a long time, people thought Japan had
around 6,800 islands. But guess what?
Scientists recently found out there are
actually 14,000 islands in Japan!

The four main islands are Hokkaido,
Honshu, Shikoku, and Kyushu.

Japan is made up of 47
prefectures*.

A prefecture is a smaller part of a country with its own
local government, similar to an American state.

Here are some facts
about Japan!

In Japanese, the name for
Japan is *Nippon* or *Nihon*.

This is our flag.

The red circle represents the
sun, because Japan is also called
the Land of the Rising Sun.

We have an Emperor and
a prime minister.

Our capital is Tokyo.

 Our currency is Yen.

"Kimigayo" is our national anthem. The lyrics are from a poem by an unknown poet, written between 900-1200 years ago.

 Sakura (cherry blossom) and chrysanthemum are our national flowers.

Japan has a national bird, the green pheasant.

NOT ME!

In Japan, people use writing systems called hiragana, katakana, and kanji.

Hiragana and katakana are like ABCs, showing how to say words.

Hiragana are used for Japanese words.

いちご
ichigo
(a strawberry)

オレンジ
orenji
(an orange)

Katakana are used for foreign words.

Kanji are like pictures, showing what words mean.

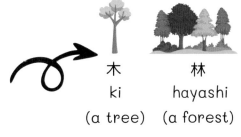

木
ki
(a tree)

林
hayashi
(a forest)

All three can be used in one sentence!

DID YOU KNOW?

There are about 2,000 kanji that people use a lot. Kids in elementary school usually learn around 1,000 kanji.

Not many people in Japan speak English, so it's a good idea to learn some Japanese before you come here!

- こんにちは konnichiwa (hello)
- おはようございます ohayo gozaimasu (good morning)
- こんばんは konbanwa (good evening)
- はい hai (yes)
- いいえ iie (no)
- ありがとう arigato (thank you)
- お願いします onegaishimasu (please)
- すみません sumimasen (excuse me)
- ごめんなさい gomen nasai (sorry)
- じゃあね jaa ne (see you)

In Japan, people bow to greet each other. There are different ways to bow, from a small head nod to a deep bend at the waist. Bowing is also used to express thanks and sorry.

Japan has a very long history.

People first came to Japan more than 30,000 years ago.

The imperial dynasty, reigned by Emperors, started between the 4th and 9th centuries, when many kingdoms and tribes decided to unite.

Around the 12th century, military rulers, called *shogun*, started to rule Japan with their army of *samurai* warriors.

In 1868, the imperial dynasty came back, marked the end of the era of the shoguns. It was known as the Meiji era. Japan became a great power.

After the World War II, Japan's economy was ruined, but the country was rebuilt and it experienced very fast economic growth after 1955.

Overall, Japan has a temperate climate, with four seasons.

However, the temperatures can vary greatly due to its long stretch from north to south.

The northern part of Japan has very cold, snowy winters and mild summers.
The average winter temperature is -6 °C (21 °F), but it can go to -30 °C (-22 °F). The average summer temperature is 20 °C (68 °F)

In central Japan, winters are milder, and summers are hot and humid.
The average temperature is 5 °C (41 °F) in winter, and 28 °C (82 °F) in summer.

The southern islands like Okinawa enjoy a subtropical climate with warm winters and hot summers.
The average temperature is 16 °C (61 °F) in winter and above 29 °C (84 °F) in summer.

8

80% of Japan is covered by mountains, and it has more than a hundred active volcanoes!

It's because Japan is located on the Pacific Ring of Fire, a path of volcanoes around the Pacific ocean.

Mount Fuji, the highest peak in Japan, is an active volcano located 100 km (62 mi) southwest of Tokyo.

Japan's location on the Pacific Ring of Fire also means that earthquakes happen a lot.

The Japanese have found ways to stay safe during an earthquake.
Most buildings are flexible so they can move along with the ground, there is an early warning system, and kids have regular earthquake drills at school.

9

Japan is home to many
native animals, such as...

Japanese macaque or
snow monkey

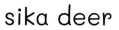

sika deer

Japanese
raccoon
dog

Japanese serow

shiba dog

koi fish

green pheasant

Japanese weasel

Japanese red fox

... and red-crown crane,
that's me!

Let's explore Japan, starting at the capital, Tokyo. We'll go up north to Sapporo, then we'll go to Kyoto, and all the way south to Okinawa.

Can't see Okinawa on this map!

The city of Tokyo is part of the huge Tokyo metropolitan area.

The Emperor and the Imperial Family live in the Imperial Palace in central Tokyo.

There are many nice areas in Tokyo to visit. Some of the most popular ones are Shibuya, Akihabara, and Asakusa.

Shibuya is great for shopping and famous for its busy crossing.

12

Akihabara is the place to be if you like anime, manga, and video games.

 You can travel back in time to old Japan in Asakusa, with its traditional shops and Senso-ji temple, a 7th century Buddhist temple.

 Now, let's go up north to the city of Sapporo in Hokkaido! In winter, it snows a lot in Sapporo.

People go to Sapporo to enjoy winter sports and to have fun at the yearly Sapporo Snow Festival.

ONSEN
(HOT SPRINGS)

There are many great places to visit just outside of Sapporo, in winter or summer.

A FLOWER FIELD
IN BIEI

13

Next, Kyoto! It's a city rich in history and culture.

You can visit many Buddhist temples in Kyoto.

KIYOMIZU-DERA TEMPLE

KINKAKU-JI TEMPLE

TOJI TEMPLE

Most temples have beautiful gardens!

GINKAKU-JI TEMPLE

TOFUKU-JI TEMPLE

FUSHIMI INARI SHRINE

Fushimi Inari Shrine is a Shinto* place of worship. It has thousands of bright orange torii gates**.

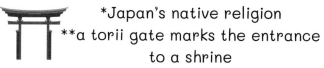

*Japan's native religion
**a torii gate marks the entrance to a shrine

Arashiyama Bamboo Forest is a great place to go for a walk!

ARASHIYAMA BAMBOO FOREST

14

Lastly, let's go all the way to Okinawa prefecture!

OKINAWA

It's in the East China Sea, quite far south from the main islands of Japan. It has more than 150 islands!

It's known for its warm, sunny subtropical climate and beautiful beaches.

MIYAKO ISLAND

You can have fun at the beach, go swimming, whale watching, fishing, and snorkeling...

You can also go hiking in the forest, exploring streams, waterfalls, and mangrove swamps.

How about going on a water buffalo cart ride? It looks really fun!

You can take the Shinkansen (bullet train) to travel all over the country.

The Shinkansen is the world's first high speed rail service. It was launched in 1964.

This was just the start of Japan's success in technology and innovation.

Japan has a big impact in the world, on everything from video games, cars, electronics, to robotics.

Nintendo, PlayStation, Sony, Toyota, Honda... they are all from Japan.

Japan is very modern and traditional at the same time.

Here are some beautiful Japanese traditions...

The Japanese tea ceremony is a special way to prepare and enjoy *matcha* (green tea).

It's held in a special tea room where everyone sits on traditional mats called *tatami*.

On May 5, Japanese people celebrate Kodomo no hi (Children's Day). Families hang *koinobori*, carp-shaped windsocks, outside their houses. Each colorful carp represents a family member. There's also a celebration just for girls, called Hinamatsuri, on March 3.

In spring, when sakura (cherry blossom) trees bloom, there's a tradition called Hanami. People all over Japan hang paper lanterns on trees and have picnics or outdoor parties.

 There are so many *matsuri* (festivals) in Japan, all year long! Some of the famous ones are...

Aomori Nebuta Matsuri, a summer festival in the city of Aomori, where you can watch a parade of colorful lantern floats.

 Kyoto Gion Matsuri, a Shinto festival of Yasaka Shrine in Kyoto, with foods, music, portable shrine processions, and parades of giant floats in the whole month of July.

Sometimes you can see people wearing *wafuku* (Japanese traditional clothing) at festivals.

KIMONO

YUKATA

Kimono is the most well-known type of *wafuku*. Yukata (casual summer wear) is another popular traditional clothing.

There are so many different types of kimono, depending on the seasons, occasions, and the wearer's age and marital status.

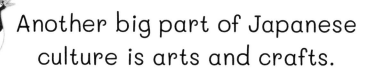

Another big part of Japanese culture is arts and crafts.

Origami is the art of folding paper to create fun and cool shapes.

Ikebana is the art of creating beautiful artwork with flowers, leaves, and branches.

Bonsai is the art of growing and shaping miniature trees in pots.

 Shodo (calligraphy) is the art of writing artistically using a brush and special ink.

Pottery is one of Japan's oldest art forms, dating back to more than 10,000 years ago.

 Manga is Japanese comics or graphic novels. It only started to be popular in 1950's, but it has roots in old Japanese art.

Anime is hand-drawn and computer-generated animation that started to be produced in Japan in the early 1900's. Studio Ghibli is probably the most famous anime studio in Japan.

Sports are also a big part
of Japanese culture.

There are a lot of sports
created or started in Japan,
mainly martial arts.

Sumo wrestling is the national
sport in Japan. It has been
practiced for centuries. There
are many ancient rituals in
sumo, such as stomping the
ground to drive away evil
spirits, rinsing the mouth with
special water, and scattering
salt to purify the space.

Judo, meaning "gentle
way" was created in the
19th century. In judo,
you learn to throw and
pin your opponents using
different techniques.

Aikido focuses on defense without hurting others. In a match, you try to redirect your opponent's energy against themselves. You can use weapons; *bokken* (wood training sword), *jo* (long staff), and *tanto* (dagger).

Kendo, meaning "the way of the sword" is a martial art where you wear armor and use bamboo swords called *shinai*.

Karate, meaning "empty hand" focuses on striking, kicking, and blocking with arms and legs. It evolved centuries ago from native martial arts in Ryukyu islands, and started to be popular in the 1900's.

In Japan, there are a lot of symbols for luck, fortune, happiness, and long life.

 Maneki-neko is a cat figurine believed to bring good luck and fortune.

Daruma dolls are for good luck and to help you achieve your goals. They are sold with blank eyes. You draw in the daruma's left eye while setting your goals. When you have achieved your goals, you can fill in the daruma's right eye.

Omamori is a small pouch with prayers written on a piece of paper inside. You can carry an omamori to protect against bad luck, attract good luck and fortune.

Senbazuru is a thousand origami cranes hung on a string. It's a symbol of long life and happiness. It's usually given to a sick person to wish them well.

23

Now, let's talk about food! YUMMY

Japanese food is famous and quite easy to find all over the world. Look at all these yummy dishes! Which ones have you tried?

SUSHI

TEMPURA

SASHIMI

Have you tried Japanese curry rice? Kids love its sweet and mild flavor.

RAMEN

UDON

SOBA

Noodles are popular in Japan. There are so many different kinds of noodles, for example *ramen* (thin, yellow noodles), *udon* (thick, chewy noodles), and *soba* (buckwheat noodles).

What do kids eat at
school in Japan?
Well, most schools in
Japan provide lunches,
but kids can also bring
their own *bento,* or
box lunches.

Kyaraben is a bento with
food arranged to look like
cute animals or popular
anime characters.

Onigiri (rice balls with
fish, pickled plum, kelp,
or other fillings) are
popular for bento.

At home, a typical meal
is rice, a main dish
(fish or other types of
protein), soup, and
pickled vegetables.

Japanese sweet treats are called *wagashi*.

DAIFUKU

SAKURA MOCHI

Mochi are sticky rice cakes. There are many types of mochi. *Daifuku* are mochi filled with sweet red bean paste. *Sakura mochi* are mochi wrapped in pickled sakura leaves.

Taiyaki are fish-shaped waffles filled with sweet red bean paste.

Amanatto are candied beans, made by boiling beans in sugar syrup, drying them, then coating them with more sugar.

Namagashi are a type of *wagashi* usually served at tea ceremonies. They are freshly made with natural ingredients.

Dango are sweet rice balls, skewered on a stick.

26

Now you know a lot about Japan! What do you think? What's the most interesting thing you learned about Japan?

BYE!
JAA NE!
じゃあね

I ❤ JAPAN

Collect all the books in the Countries for Kiddies series!

countries-for-kiddies.com